D1288471

THE CHILDREN'S BIBLE

Volume 9

A Golden Press / Funk & Wagnalls, Inc. Book
Published by Western Publishing Company, Inc.

COPYRIGHT © 1981, 1965 BY WESTERN PUBLISHING COMPANY, INC. COPYRIGHT © 1962 BY FRATELLI FAB-
BRI, MILAN, ALL RIGHTS RESERVED. PRINTED IN THE U.S.A. PUBLISHED BY GOLDEN PRESS, NEW YORK,
BY ARRANGEMENT WITH WESTERN PUBLISHING—HACHETTE INTERNATIONAL, S.A., GENEVA.
GOLDEN® AND GOLDEN PRESS® are trademarks of Western Publishing Company, Inc.

Classic™ binding
R. R. Donnelley & Sons Company
patents--U.S. pending
Distributed by Funk & Wagnalls, Inc. New York
Library of Congress Catalog Card Number: 81-81439

ISBN 0-8343-0046-X (Volume 9)
ISBN 0-8343-0037-0 (12 Volume Set)

CONTENTS

ZACHARIAS AND ELISABETH   526
Zacharias is made speechless because he doubts that God is
sending him a son.

AN ANGEL VISITS MARY   528
The angel Gabriel tells Mary that she will bear a holy child who
shall be called the Son of God.

THE BIRTH OF JESUS   531
Jesus is born in a stable in Bethlehem.

THE VISIT OF THE WISE MEN   534
King Herod sends wise men from the East to seek out the
baby Jesus for him.

THE FLIGHT INTO EGYPT   536
God warns Mary and Joseph to flee Palestine because King Herod
is planning to kill Jesus.

JESUS AMONG THE TEACHERS   538
Jesus astounds the religious teachers and leaders of the temple
with his understanding and knowledge.

THE BAPTISM OF JESUS BY JOHN   540
The spirit of God comes to Jesus after he is baptised by John the
Baptist.

THE TEMPTATION IN THE WILDERNESS   542
Satan tries to convince Jesus to sin.

JESUS IN GALILEE   544
Jesus chooses four fishermen as his first disciples.

THE MARRIAGE IN CANA   546
At a wedding feast, Jesus turns water into wine.

JESUS PREACHES IN THE SYNAGOGUES   548
Jesus' fame as a healer spreads throughout Galilee after he heals a
man in the synagogue.

THE PHARISEES QUESTION JESUS   550
The authorities persecute Jesus because he healed people on the
Sabbath.

THE SERMON ON THE MOUNT   556
Jesus teaches his many disciples what they must do to follow God's
wishes.

THE MINISTRY OF JESUS CONTINUES   564
Jesus raises a boy from the dead and the people proclaim him
a great prophet.

ILLUSTRATED GLOSSARY   568
Notes, definitions, illustrations, and maps.

THE
NEW TESTAMENT

INTRODUCTION

Matthew, Mark, Luke, and John, the four Gospels of the New Testament, recount the story of Jesus of Nazareth. Christians believe that Jesus was the Messiah that the prophets in the Old Testament said God would send to his people. Messiah means "anointed one." The name Christ comes from *christos*, the Greek word for Messiah.

Many of the Jews at the time of Jesus were hoping for a Messiah who would free them from foreign rule. The Jews believed that a Messiah would be specially chosen by God to reestablish the nation of Israel. The people believed that when the Messiah came, Israel would become a new kind of nation. The Messiah would bring peace and prosperity to the land. Once again the poor would receive justice from the courts, because God's laws would be supreme. The Lord would invite all men and women of the world into this new life that the Messiah would bring. Sometimes the Jews even spoke about this new Israel as the return of paradise to Earth.

Ever since the time of their exile in Babylon, the Jewish people had longed for a brave and powerful warrior like King David—a Messiah who would free them from the heathen who ruled Palestine. They remembered that God had promised Abraham that the land of Canaan would forever belong to his descendants. The Jews also remembered the glory of King David's reign, when Israel had been one of the most powerful nations of the world. They remembered these things and longed to be free again on their own land and with their own king.

From the time of Ezra and Nehemiah until the time of Jesus, many different nations ruled over Israel. During this time, the Jews were almost never free. They were able to remain faithful to their customs and to follow the laws that Ezra had given them, but the independent nation of Israel did not exist anymore. Until 334 B.C., Palestine was part of the great Persian Empire. The Persian rulers allowed the Jews much freedom in governing themselves. Judah was ruled by high priests in Jerusalem. The Israelites were allowed to make their own coins and they collected their own taxes. This period under Persian rule was not a bad time for the people of Israel.

In 334 B.C., Alexander the Great, who was the ruler of Greece, defeated the Persians and began to take over their empire. By the year 332 B.C., the people of Israel had also become part of his empire. Alexander the Great was a young man when he began to build his empire. He was a great general and soon his empire stretched from Greece all the way to India. There is a legend that says when Alexander reached India he cried because there were no more lands for him to conquer.

For many years the Greeks allowed the Jews to worship God and to govern themselves, though they wanted the people they conquered to adopt Greek customs and culture. Some of the Greeks wanted the Jews to worship Zeus, the great Greek God, along with their own Lord. The Jews, however, would worship only the one God. Every Sabbath they gathered in the synagogues in their towns to pray and study the Scriptures. The synagogue was the place of worship, the school and the local meeting place of the Jews. It was also the center of each town.

After Alexander's death, the Greek Empire was divided among his generals. Seleucus became ruler of the eastern part of the empire, which included Syria and Babylon. Ptolemy ruled over Egypt. The two rulers fought for control of Palestine, and Ptolemy gained control in 301 B.C. He and his successors allowed the Jews to practice their religion freely. But the successors of Seleucus, who took Palestine away from Ptolemy VI in 198 B.C., began a much harsher treatment of the Jews.

At first the Seleucids allowed the Jews to govern themselves, just as the Persians and the Ptolemies had done. But when the Seleucid rulers needed a great deal of money to pay tribute to the Romans, they began to tax the people of Israel very heavily. They also stole gold and jewels from the temple. The Jews protested loudly.

Then in 167 B.C., the Seleucid king, Antiochus Epiphanes, sent his armies into Jerusalem to punish the people. They killed many of the inhabitants of the city, tore down the city walls, and set up an army camp right in Jerusalem. They even took over the temple and made an altar to Zeus where the altar to the Lord had been. They outraged the Jews by killing a pig and eating its meat, a food strictly forbidden by Mosaic Law, right in the temple.

The angered Jews rose up in rebellion against the Seleucids. Their fighters were led by a great leader, Judas Maccabeus, who reminded the people of the judges of Israel's past. Judas defeated the Seleucid troops. In 164 B.C., he reclaimed the temple and cleaned it out. Judas rededicated the temple to the Lord and the people of Jerusalem sang and danced for joy in the streets. Jewish people still remember and celebrate this event during the feast of Chanukah.

The Maccabees did not completely free Palestine from Seleucid control, but they did win back the right of the Jewish people to govern themselves. The Maccabees and their descendants, who are called the Hasmonean Kings, ruled over Judah for about a century. Under the Hasmoneans, the Jews enjoyed a measure of independence for the first time in many years. Once again the Jewish people began to think of David and to long for the return of the nation of Israel.

This did not happen, however. One of the most powerful empires ever to exist, the Roman Empire, was now dominating the world. The armies of Rome had already conquered much of the land around Palestine by the time of the Hasmoneans. The Jewish kings tried to stay friendly with Rome. Unfortunately, the Hasmoneans began to fight among themselves and so they weakened the unity of the Jews. Rome used this opportunity to capture Judah. In 63 B.C., the Romans invaded Palestine and made it part of the great Roman Empire. Although they allowed the Jews to rule themselves, they demanded obedience to Rome. Once again the Jewish people were ruled by a powerful foreign government. There was often great hatred and tension between the Romans and the Jews.

Throughout this long and hard history the Jewish people remained faithful to the Lord. Judah suffered much from the greed and hatred of other nations, but the Jews never forgot their God. The people prayed to God to send a Messiah as the Old Testament had promised. They hoped he would free them from Roman rule.

Jesus was born during this time of Roman rule. He was born to a poor family from the town of Nazareth in Galilee. The New Testament tells us that a young woman named Mary was Jesus' mother. God gave Mary a wonderful and special gift— God asked Mary to be the mother of his son. He asked Mary and her husband, Joseph, to raise Jesus as their son.

Mary and Joseph were poor people. Joseph was a carpenter who made wooden cabinets for the people of Nazareth. He taught Jesus how to be a carpenter, too. The New Testament tells us that Jesus left his home when he was a young man to teach the people of Israel about God's love for them. But he never forgot the people he lived with and worked among in Nazareth. Jesus always had a special love for the poor. His love for the poor was like God's love for the widows, orphans, and needy that was expressed in the Old Testament.

When Jesus began to preach in public, some people thought that he would lead the Jews in rebellion against the Romans. Many of his followers thought that he was the warrior and king the Jews had been awaiting for so long. Jesus had to teach his followers that he was not this kind of Messiah. In the

Sermon on the Mount, Jesus taught his disciples that he was a Messiah of gentleness and poverty. He had come to free the people not from the Romans, but from their sins and their sorrow. Jesus tried to teach his followers that they too had to depend on God as the poor, the weak, and the suffering depended on him.

The Gospels of Matthew, Mark, Luke, and John tell the story of Jesus of Nazareth. "Gospel" means "good news." The story of Jesus' life, which you will read about in *The Children's Bible*, is the good news that Christians want to tell everyone about. They say that all men and women can be happy and hopeful now that Jesus has lived. This is why Christians wrote the Gospels.

Even before the Gospels were written, men and women who believed in Jesus collected stories about him. They talked to each other about him. They wanted to remember how he had told them to live. For a long time, Christians proclaimed the good news by preaching and teaching. The Gospels were written many years after Jesus' death. The first Gospel to be written down was the Gospel of Mark. Matthew and Luke came next, and the Gospel of John was the last one to be written down.

According to tradition, the four Gospels were written by Matthew, Mark, Luke, and John, who were disciples or early apostles. Because the Gospels were written by four different people, each tells the stories in a different way. Matthew was a former tax-collector and one of Jesus' disciples. He wrote his Gospel to tell the story of Jesus to the early Christians, especially to those who had been Jews. Mark was a friend and helper of the disciples Peter and Paul, and he also wrote for people who wanted to learn more about Jesus. Luke was a friend and companion of Paul and wrote primarily for Christians who had not been Jewish. John was Jesus' most beloved disciple. He wrote to tell all men and women that Jesus was the Messiah that the Jewish people had long been waiting for.

Christians say that God wanted men and women to know how much he loved them, so he sent his only son to tell everyone about his love. He sent his son to show them how to love God in return and how to respect each other. Christians say that before Jesus was born, the world was a sad place. It was as if God was on one side of a river and men and women were on the other side. They did not know how to get across. Jesus is the bridge between them. And at the same time, he is waiting for them on the other side. At last men and women had a way to reach God. This is why the angels told the shepherds they should feel great joy that Jesus was born.

from the
BOOKS OF
MATTHEW, MARK,
LUKE, and JOHN

ZACHARIAS AND ELISABETH

T HERE was in the days of Herod, the king of Judea, a priest named Zacharias, and his wife Elisabeth. They were both righteous before God, keeping the commandments of the Lord. But they had no children, and they were both well advanced in years.

Now when it was Zacharias' turn to serve in the temple, he went into the temple to burn incense while the whole multitude of the people prayed outside. And an angel of the Lord appeared to him at the right side of the altar, and when Zacharias saw him, he was troubled and fear fell upon him. But the angel said to him:

"Fear not, Zacharias, for your prayer is heard. Your wife shall bear you a son, and you shall call his name John. You shall have joy and gladness and many shall rejoice at his birth. For he shall be great in the sight of the Lord, and shall drink neither wine nor strong drink. He shall be filled with the Holy Spirit. And he shall turn many of the children of Israel to the Lord their God.

"He shall go before him in the spirit and power of Elijah, to turn the hearts of the fathers to the children, and the disobedient to the wisdom of the just, to make ready a people prepared for the Lord."

"How am I to know this is to be?" said Zacharias to the angel. "For I am an old man and my wife too is advanced in years."

The angel answered him, saying:

"I am Gabriel, and I stand in the presence of God. I have been sent to speak to you and to tell you these glad tidings. And, behold, you shall be dumb and unable to speak until these things come about, because you did not believe my words."

The people waiting outside wondered why Zacharias was so long in

the temple. When he came out he could not speak to them, and they sensed that he had seen a vision in the temple, for he made signs to them and remained speechless.

And when his time of service was completed he returned home, and before long his wife Elisabeth knew that she was going to have a child.

AN ANGEL
VISITS MARY

HE angel Gabriel was sent by God to a city of Galilee named Nazareth, to a maiden betrothed to a man named Joseph, of the family of David. The name of the maiden was Mary.

The angel appeared to her and said:

"Hail, you who are highly favored! The Lord is with you; blessed are you among women."

And when she saw him, she was troubled at what he had said and wondered to herself what this greeting could mean. Then the angel continued:

"Fear not, Mary, for you have found favor with God. You shall bring forth a son and shall call his name Jesus. He shall be great, and shall be called the Son of the Highest, and the Lord God shall give him the throne of his forefather David. He shall rule over the house of Jacob for ever, and of his kingdom there shall be no end."

"How shall this be," Mary said to the angel, "seeing that I have no husband?"

The angel answered and said to her:

"The Holy Spirit shall come upon you and the power of the Most High shall overshadow you. The child that is born of you shall be holy and shall be called the Son of God."

"Behold, I am the handmaiden of the Lord," Mary said. "Let it be to me as you have said."

So Mary arose and went into the hill country with haste, to a town of Judah where she went to the house of Zacharias and his wife, her cousin Elisabeth. And when Elisabeth heard her greeting she was filled with the Holy Spirit and she cried out with a loud voice:

"Blessed are you among women, and blessed is the child you shall bear. But why is it that the mother of my Lord should come to me?"

And Mary said:

"My soul does praise the Lord,
And my spirit has rejoiced
* in God my Savior.*
For he has regarded the lowliness
* of his handmaiden: for, behold,*
* from henceforth all generations*
* shall call me blessed:*
For he that is mighty has done
* great things for me,*
* and holy is his name.*
His mercy is on those who fear him
* from generation to generation.*
He has showed strength with his arm;
* he has scattered the proud*
* in the imagination of their hearts.*

He has put down the mighty
* from their thrones and*
* has exalted them of low degree.*
He has filled the hungry
* with good things,*
* and the rich he has sent*
* empty away.*
He has helped his servant Israel,
* in remembrance of his mercy;*
As he spoke to our fathers,
* to Abraham, and to his seed for ever."*

Mary remained with Elisabeth for about three months and then returned to her own house.

THE BIRTH OF JOHN THE BAPTIST

Now Elisabeth's time came that she should give birth, and she brought forth a son. Her neighbors and her cousins heard how the Lord had shown great mercy upon her, and they rejoiced with her.

And it came to pass that on the eighth day the child was to be circumcised, and they called him Zacharias after the name of his father.

But his mother said, "No, he shall be called John." And they said to her, "There is no one of your family that is called by this name." And they made signs to his father, asking how he would have him called.

Zacharias asked for a writing table, and wrote: "His name is John." And they all marveled. Then immediately Zacharias' mouth was opened, and his tongue loosed, and he spoke and praised God. And fear came on all that lived round about them.

Word of all these doings spread throughout all the hill country of Judah, and all that heard of them laid them up in their hearts, saying:

"What kind of child shall this be!"

And his father Zacharias was filled with the Holy Spirit, and prophesied, saying:

"Blessed be the Lord of Israel,
for he has visited and
redeemed his people,
And has raised up a horn
of salvation for us
in the house of his servant David
As he spoke by the mouth
of his holy prophets,
which have been since
the world began:
That we may be saved from our enemies,
and from the hand of all that hate us,
To perform the mercy promised
to our fathers, and
to remember his holy covenant;
The oath which he swore
to our father Abraham,
That he would grant unto us,
that we being delivered
out of the hand of our enemies,
might serve him without fear,
In holiness and righteousness
before him, all the days of our life:
And you, child, shall be called
the prophet of the Highest,
for you shall go before the face
of the Lord to prepare his ways:
To give knowledge of salvation
to his people by remission
of their sins, through the
tender mercy of our God;
whereby the dayspring from
on high has visited us,
To give light to them that sit
in darkness and in the shadow
of death, to guide our feet
into the way of peace."

The child grew and became strong in spirit, and lived in the deserts till the day of his appearance unto Israel.

THE BIRTH OF JESUS

T came to pass in those days that a decree went out from Caesar Augustus, the emperor in Rome, that all the world should be taxed. This taxing was first made when Cyrenius was governor of Syria.

Everyone went to be taxed, each to his own city. And Joseph went up from Galilee, from the city of Nazareth, into Judea, to the city of David which is called Bethlehem, because he was of the house and family of David, to be taxed with Mary his wife who was soon to have a child.

So it came to pass that while they were there the day arrived for her child to be born. She brought forth her firstborn son, and wrapped him in swaddling clothes, and laid him in a manger, because there was no room for them in the inn.

There were in the same country shepherds staying in the field, keeping watch over their flocks by night. And lo, the angel of the Lord came upon them, and the glory of the Lord shone round about them, and they were much afraid.

"Fear not," the angel said to them. "For I bring you good tidings of a great joy that is coming to all people. For to you is born this day in the city of David a Savior who is Christ the Lord. And this shall be a sign to you: You shall find the babe wrapped in swaddling clothes, lying in a manger."

And suddenly there was with the angel a multitude of the heavenly host praising God and saying:

"Glory to God in the highest,
and on earth peace,
good will toward men."

When the angels had gone away from them into heaven, the shepherds

said to one another, "Let us go into Bethlehem and see this thing which has come to pass, which the Lord has made known to us."

They went with haste and found Mary and Joseph, and the babe lying in a manger. And when they had seen it, they made known throughout the land what they had been told concerning this child. And all who heard it marveled at the things which were told them by the shepherds. But Mary kept all these things, and pondered them in her heart.

THE PRESENTATION IN THE TEMPLE

Now when the time arrived for the child to be circumcised, he was called Jesus, the name given him by the angel before he was born. And when the days of the purification were over, according to the law of Moses, they brought him to Jerusalem, to present him to the Lord (as it is written in the law of the Lord, "Every firstborn son shall be called holy to the Lord") and to offer a sacrifice according to that which is said in the law of the Lord: "A pair of turtledoves or two young pigeons."

And there was a man in Jerusalem whose name was Simeon, and who was just and devout. The Holy Spirit was in him, and had revealed to him that he should not die before he had seen the Lord's Christ. The Spirit led him that day to the temple, and when the parents brought in the child Jesus, to do for him what the law required, Simeon took him up in his arms, and blessed God and said:

"Lord, now let your servant depart
  in peace, according to your word.
For my eyes have seen your salvation,
  which you have prepared before
  the face of all people;
A light to lighten the Gentiles,
  and the glory of your people Israel."

Joseph and the child's mother marveled at the things which were spoken of him. And Simeon blessed them, and said to Mary. "This child is destined to bring about the fall and rising again of many in Israel. He shall be a sign against which many shall speak (yes, through him a sword shall pierce your own soul also) that the thoughts of many hearts may be revealed."

THE VISIT
OF THE
WISE MEN

OW when Jesus was born in Bethlehem of Judea, in the days of Herod the king, there came wise men from the east to Jerusalem, asking: "Where is he that is born King of the Jews? For we have seen his star in the east and are come to worship him."

When Herod the king heard these things, he was troubled, and all Jerusalem with him. And when he had gathered all the chief priests and scribes of the people together, he asked them where Christ should be born. "In Bethlehem of Judea," they said. "For thus it is written by the prophet:

'*And you, Bethlehem, in the land of Judah,*
are not the least among
the princes of Judah.
For out of you shall come a Governor,
that shall rule my people Israel.' "

Then Herod sent secretly for the wise men, and asked them what time the star had appeared. And he sent them to Bethlehem, saying, "Go and search carefully for the young child, and when you have found him, bring me word, that I may come and worship him also."

When they had heard the king, they departed. And, lo, the star which they saw in the east went before them till it came and stood over the place where the young child was. When they saw the star, they rejoiced with

great joy. And when they came into the house, they saw the young child with Mary his mother, and they fell down and worshiped him, and presented to him gifts: gold, frankincense, and myrrh. And being warned by God in a dream that they should not return to Herod, they departed and returned to their own country by another way.

THE FLIGHT INTO EGYPT

WHEN the wise men had departed, the angel of the Lord appeared and spoke to Joseph in a dream, saying:

"Arise, and take the young child and his mother, and flee into Egypt, and stay there until I bring you word. For Herod will seek the child to destroy him."

So he arose and took the young child and his mother into Egypt. And there they remained until the death of Herod, that the word of the prophet of the Lord might be fulfilled: "Out of Egypt have I called my son."

When Herod saw that the wise men had deceived him, he was greatly angered. He ordered that all the children under two years old in Bethlehem and the land around should be put to death, in accordance with the time he had learned from the wise men. Then was fulfilled that which was spoken by Jeremiah the prophet:

"*In Rama was there a voice heard,*
   lamenting, and weeping and mourning,
Rachel weeping for her children,
   and would not be comforted,
   because they were no more."

But when Herod died, an angel of the Lord appeared in a dream to Joseph in Egypt, saying: "Rise up and take the young child and his mother and go into the land of Israel. For those who sought the child's life are dead."

And he arose and took the young child and his mother, and went into the land of Israel. But when he heard that Archelaus reigned in Judea in the place of his father Herod, he was afraid to go there. So, being warned by God in a dream, he turned aside again into the region of Galilee. He went and settled in the city of Nazareth, so that the words which were spoken by the prophets might be fulfilled: "He shall be called a Nazarene."

JESUS AMONG THE TEACHERS

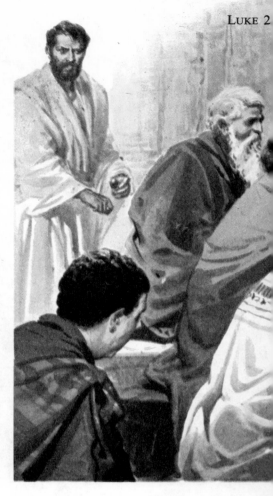

ND the child grew and became strong in spirit and filled with wisdom, and the grace of God was upon him.

Now when he was twelve years old, his parents went up to Jerusalem according to the custom for the feast of the passover. After the passover was ended, and they were returning, the child Jesus stayed behind in Jerusalem.

Joseph and Mary did not know this and, supposing him to have been in their group, went a day's journey before seeking him among their kinsmen and acquaintances. When they did not find him, they turned back again to Jerusalem, seeking him.

After three days, they found him in the temple, sitting among the teachers, both listening to them and asking them questions. And all who heard him were astonished at his understanding and answers.

When his parents saw him, they were amazed. And his mother said to him, "Son, why have you behaved like this to us? Your father and I have been

looking for you and worrying." And he said to them, "Why did you look for me? Did you not know that I must be about my Father's business?" But they did not understand what he was saying to them.

Then he went with them to Nazareth, and was obedient to them, but his mother kept all these things in her heart. Jesus, as he grew up, increased both in wisdom and in favor with God and man.

THE BAPTISM OF JESUS BY JOHN

OW in the fifteenth year of the reign of Tiberius Caesar, when Pontius Pilate was governor of Judea, and Herod was tetrarch of Galilee, the word of God came unto John the son of Zacharias in the wilderness. And he came into all the country about Jordan, preaching the baptism of repentance for the remission of sins, as it is written in the book of Isaiah the prophet, saying:

"The voice of one crying in the wilderness,
'Prepare ye the way of the Lord,
* make his paths straight.*
Every valley shall be filled,
* and every mountain*
* and hill shall be made low.*
And the crooked shall be made straight,
* and the rough shall be made smooth.*
And all flesh shall see
* the salvation of God.' "*

John wore clothing made of camel's hair, and a leather girdle about his waist. And his food was locusts and wild honey.

The people of Jerusalem and all Judea and all the region round about Jordan, went out to him, and were baptized by him, confessing their sins. But when he saw many of the Pharisees and Sadducees come to his baptism, he said to them:

"O generation of vipers, who has warned you to flee from the wrath to come? Do, therefore, deeds that show repentance, and do not just say within yourselves, 'We have Abraham for

forth good fruit is cut down and cast into the fire."

"What shall we do then?" the people asked him. And he answered:

"He who has two coats, let him give to him who has none, and he who has meat, let him give to those that are without."

Then came also tax-collectors to be baptized and said to him, "Master, what shall we do?" And he said to them, "Collect no more than you are instructed to."

Soldiers came to him asking, "And what shall we do?" And he said to them, "Do violence to no man, nor accuse any falsely. And be content with your wages."

People were expectant and wondered in their hearts whether he was the Christ or not. John therefore answered, saying to all of them:

"I indeed baptize you with water, but one mightier than I is coming whose shoes I am not worthy to undo. He shall baptize you with the Holy Spirit and with fire.

"His fork is in his hand, and he will thoroughly clean his floor after the harvest, and will gather his wheat into the granary. But he will burn up the chaff with unquenchable fire."

Then Jesus came from Galilee to Jordan in order to be baptized by John. But John stopped him saying, "I have need to be baptized by you, and do you come to me?"

And Jesus answering said to him, "Let it be so now, for by us must all righteousness be fulfilled."

So John consented. And Jesus, when he was baptized, arose directly from the water. And, lo, the heavens were opened and he saw the Spirit of God coming down like a dove, and alighting upon him. And behold a voice from heaven said:

"This is my beloved Son, in whom I am well pleased."

our forefather.' For I say to you that God is able to raise up children for Abraham from these stones. And now the axe is laid to the root of the trees. Therefore, every tree which brings not

THE TEMPTATION IN THE WILDERNESS

 JESUS, full of the Holy Spirit, returned from the Jordan and was led by the Spirit into the wilderness to be tempted by the devil. Jesus fasted forty days and forty nights, and afterwards he was hungry. Then the devil came to him and said, "If you are the Son of God, command that these stones be made bread."

But Jesus answered saying:

"It is written: Man shall not live by bread alone, but by every word that comes out of the mouth of God."

Then the devil took him up into the holy city, and set him on a pinnacle of the temple, and said to him, "If you are the Son of God, throw yourself down. For it is written that he shall put his angels in charge of you to keep you safe, and they shall catch you in their hands, lest you strike your foot against a stone." Jesus said to him:

"It is written also: You shall not tempt the Lord your God."

Again, the devil took him up into a very big mountain, and showed him all the kingdoms of the world, and the glory of them. And he said:

"All these things I will give you, if you will fall down and worship me."

Then Jesus said:

"Away, Satan. For it is written: You shall worship the Lord your God, and him only shall you serve."

Then the devil left him and, behold, angels came and ministered unto him.

JESUS
IN
GALILEE

 NOW Herod, being reproved by John for all the evils which he had done, had John cast into prison, and when Jesus heard this, he departed into Galilee. And leaving Nazareth, he came and dwelt in Capernaum which is on the sea coast.

At this time Jesus began to preach, and to say, "Repent, for the kingdom of heaven is at hand." He was about thirty years of age when he began his ministry.

And as he was walking by the sea of Galilee, he saw Simon and Andrew his brother casting a net into the sea, for they were fishermen. And he went onto one of the boats, which was Simon's, and asked him to push out a little from the shore. Then he sat down and taught the people from the boat.

When he had finished speaking, he said to Simon, "Launch out into the deep water and let down your nets for a catch." And Simon answering said to him, "Master, we have labored all night and have taken nothing. Nevertheless, at your word I will let down the nets."

When they had done this, they enclosed a great multitude of fish, and their nets broke. Then they called their partners, who were in another boat, that they should come and help them. And they came, and filled both the boats so full that they began to sink.

When Simon saw this, he fell down at Jesus' knees, saying, "Depart from me, for I am a sinful man, O Lord." For he was astonished, and so were all that were with him, at the catch of fish which they had taken.

Then Jesus said to them, "Follow me, and I will make you fishers of men." And immediately they forsook their nets, and followed him.

When he had gone a little further, he saw James the son of Zebedee, and John his brother, who were in their boat mending their nets. He called them, and they left their father Zebedee in the boat with the hired servants, and followed him.

THE MARRIAGE IN CANA

T HE third day there was a marriage in Cana of Galilee, and the mother of Jesus was there. Jesus and his disciples were also invited to the wedding. And when they wanted wine, the mother of Jesus said to him, "They have no more wine." Jesus said to her, "Woman, what would you have me do? It is not yet time for me to act." His mother said to the servants, "Whatever he says to you, do it."

Now there were six stone waterpots standing there for the purification rites of the Jews, holding twenty to thirty gallons apiece. Jesus said to the servants, "Fill the waterpots with water." And they filled them to the brim. Then he said to them, "Draw some out now, and take it to the master of the feast." And they took it.

When the master of the feast tasted the water that was made wine, not knowing where it came from (but the servants who had drawn the water knew), the master of the feast called to the bridegroom and said to him, "Every man sets out good wine at the beginning, and when men have drunk well, then that which is worse. But you have kept the good wine until now."

This beginning of miracles Jesus did in Cana of Galilee, and showed his glory, and his disciples believed in him.

546

JESUS PREACHES IN THE SYNAGOGUES

AFTER this he went down to Capernaum, with his mother and his brothers and his disciples, and on the sabbath day he entered into the synagogue and taught. And people were astonished at his words, for he taught them as one that had authority, and not as the scribes.

And there was in the synagogue a man with an unclean spirit and he cried out saying:

"Let us alone. What have we to do with you, Jesus of Nazareth? Have you come to destroy us? I know who you are: the Holy One of God."

And Jesus rebuked him saying, "Hold your peace, and come out of him."

The unclean spirit shook him and cried with a loud voice, and then came out of him. And they were all amazed, and they questioned among themselves, saying, "What thing is this? What new doctrine is this? For with authority he commands even the unclean spirits and they do obey him." And immediately his fame spread abroad throughout all the region round about Galilee.

When they left the synagogue, they went into the house of Simon and Andrew, with James and John. Simon's

wife's mother lay sick of a fever, and they told him of her. And he came and took her by the hand, and lifted her up, and immediately the fever left her, and she waited upon them.

That evening, when the sun did set they brought to him all that were diseased and them that were possessed with devils. And all the city was gathered together at the door. He healed many that were sick of various diseases, and cast out many devils.

In the morning, rising up a long while before daylight, he went out and departed into a solitary place, and there prayed. Simon and they that were with him followed after him, and when they found him, they said to him, "All men seek for you." And he said to them, "Let us go into the next towns, that I may preach there also, for that is why I came forth."

And he preached in synagogues throughout all Galilee, and cast out devils.

JESUS HEALS THE LEPER

And there came a leper to him, begging him, and kneeling down and saying to him:

"If you will, you can make me clean."

Jesus, moved with compassion, put forth his hand, and touched him, and said to him, "I will. Be clean." And as soon as he had spoken, immediately the leprosy departed from him, and he was cleansed. Then he sent him away, saying to him, "See that you say nothing to any man, but go your way, show yourself to the priest, and offer for your cleansing those things which Moses commanded."

But he went out and told the news widely, so much that Jesus could no longer openly enter into the city, but stayed outside in desert places. And people came to him from every quarter.

THE PHARISEES QUESTION JESUS

IT came to pass on a certain day, as he was teaching, that there were Pharisees and doctors of the law sitting by, who had come out of every town of Galilee, and Judea, and Jerusalem. And the power of the Lord was present to heal them.

Some men brought in a bed a man who was taken with a paralysis. They sought means to bring him in and lay him before Jesus, but they could not find a way because of the multitude. So they went upon a housetop and let him down through the roof with the bed into the presence of Jesus. And when Jesus saw their faith, he said to him, "Man, your sins are forgiven you."

Then the scribes and the Pharisees began questioning, saying, "Who is this who speaks blasphemies? Who can forgive sins, but God alone?"

But when Jesus sensed what they were thinking, he answered them, and said:

"Why do you question in your hearts, asking whether it is easier to say, 'Your sins are forgiven you,' or 'Rise up and walk'?

"In order that you may know that the Son of man has power on earth to forgive sins," (he said to the paralyzed man), "I say to you: Arise, and take up your bed and go into your house."

And immediately he rose up before them, and took up the bed on which he lay, and departed to his own house, glorifying God. And they were all amazed, and they glorified God, and were filled with fear, saying, "We have seen strange things today."

As Jesus went on his way, he saw a man named Matthew sitting at the tax office, and he said to him, "Follow me." And Matthew arose and followed him.

550

One day, as Jesus sat eating, many tax-collectors and sinners came and sat down with him and his disciples. And when the Pharisees saw it, they said to his disciples, "Why does your master eat with tax-collectors and sinners?"

And Jesus, answering, said to them:

"They that are healthy do not need a physician, but they that are sick. Go and learn what this means: 'I will have mercy, and not sacrifice.' For I have not come to call the righteous, but sinners to repentance."

Then the disciples of John came to him, saying, "Why do we and the Pharisees fast often, while your disciples do not fast?"

And Jesus said to them:

"Do wedding guests mourn, as long as the bridegroom is with them? The days will come when the bridegroom shall be taken from them, and then they shall fast."

THE SABBATH DAY

At that time Jesus went on the sabbath day through the corn. His disciples were hungry and began to pluck ears of corn, and to eat. When the Pharisees saw it, they said to him, "Behold, your disciples are doing what it is not lawful to do upon the sabbath day."

But he said to them:

"Have you not read what David did, and those who were with him, when he was hungry: how he entered into the house of God and ate the showbread, which was not lawful for him to eat, nor for those who were with him, but only for the priests?

"Or have you not read in the law, how on the sabbath days the priests in the temple profane the sabbath and are blameless? But I say to you that in this place is one greater than the temple. For the Son of man is Lord even of the sabbath day."

JESUS HEALS ON THE SABBATH

And he went out from there and went into their synagogue where there was a man who had his hand withered. And they asked him, "Is it lawful to heal on the sabbath day?" so that they might accuse him.

Then Jesus said to them:

"What man is there among you that, if he has a sheep that falls into a pit on the sabbath day, will not take hold of it and lift it out? How much better is a man than a sheep? It is therefore lawful to do good on the sabbath."

Then he said to the man, "Stretch forth your hand." And he stretched it forth and it was restored whole like the other. Then the Pharisees went

out, and held a meeting against him, to plan how they might destroy him.

Now there is at Jerusalem by the sheep market a pool. Around it lay a great multitude of invalid folk, of blind, lame and withered, waiting for the water to move. For an angel of the

Lord went down at certain seasons into the pool and troubled the water. And whoever stepped in first after the troubling of the water was cured of whatever disease he had.

THE INVALID AT THE POOL

A certain man was there who had had a sickness for thirty-eight years. When Jesus saw him and knew that he had been lying there a long time, he said to him, "Do you wish to be made healthy?"

The invalid man answered, "Sir, I have no man to put me in the pool when the water is troubled, and while I am going, another steps down before me."

is not lawful for you to carry your bed." He answered them, "He that made me healthy said to me, 'Take up your bed and walk.' "

Then they asked him, "What man is the one who said to you, 'Take up your bed and walk?' " But he that was healed did not know who it was, for Jesus had gone away, a crowd being in the place.

Afterward, Jesus found him in the temple, and said to him, "Behold, you are well. Sin no more, lest a worse thing come to you." The man departed, and told the priests that it was Jesus who had healed him. And therefore the authorities persecuted Jesus, and tried to slay him, because he had done these things on the sabbath day.

Jesus said to him, "Rise, take up your bed, and walk." And immediately the man was made healthy, and took up his bed, and walked.

Now that day was the sabbath. Therefore the Jews said to him that was cured, "It is the sabbath day. It

But Jesus answered them, "My Father is forever at work, and so am I." Therefore his enemies tried even more to kill him, because he not only had broken the sabbath, but said also that God was his Father, making himself equal with God.

THE TWELVE APOSTLES ARE CHOSEN

And it came to pass in those days that he went out into a mountain to pray, and continued all night in prayer to God. And when it was day, he called to him his disciples, and of them he chose twelve, whom he also named apostles. And he gave to them power to cast out unclean spirits, and to heal all kinds of sickness and all disease.

Now the names of the twelve apostles are these: The first, Simon, who is called Peter, and Andrew his brother; James the son of Zebedee and John his brother; Philip and Bartholomew; Thomas and Matthew the publican; James the son of Alpheus and Lebbeus, whose surname was Thaddeus; Simon the Canaanite; and Judas Iscariot, who betrayed him.

And he came down with them, and stood in the plain, with the company of his disciples and a great multitude of people from all Judea and Jerusalem, and from the sea coast of Tyre and Sidon, which came to hear him and to be healed from their diseases. And they that were troubled with unclean spirits were healed. And the whole multitude tried to touch him, for goodness went forth from him and healed every one of them.

555

THE SERMON ON THE MOUNT

ND seeing the multitudes, he went up into a mountain. And when he had found a suitable place, his disciples came to him, and he opened his mouth and taught them saying:

"Blessed are the poor in spirit,
for theirs is the kingdom of heaven.
Blessed are they that mourn,
for they shall be comforted.
Blessed are the meek,
for they shall inherit the earth.
Blessed are they which do hunger
and thirst for righteousness,
for they shall be filled.
Blessed are the merciful,
for they shall obtain mercy.
Blessed are the pure in heart,
for they shall see God.
Blessed are the peacemakers,
for they shall be called
the children of God.
Blessed are they which are persecuted
for righteousness' sake,
for theirs is the kingdom of heaven.
Blessed are you, when men
shall revile you, and persecute you,
and shall say all manner of evil
against you falsely, for my sake.
Rejoice, and be exceeding glad,
for great is your reward in heaven,
for so persecuted they the prophets
which were before you.

"You are the salt of the earth. But if the salt has lost its flavor, how shall it be salty again? It is then fit for nothing but to be thrown out and trodden underfoot.

"You are the light of the world. A city that is set on a hill cannot be hidden.

"Men do not light a candle and put it under a bushel, but on a candlestick, where it gives light to all that are in the house.

"Let your light so shine before men that they may see your good works and glorify your Father who is in heaven.

THE LAW AND THE PROPHETS

"Do not think that I have come to destroy the old law or the prophets. I have not come to destroy but to fulfill. For truly I say to you, till heaven and earth pass away, not one dotting of an 'i' nor crossing of a 't' will be removed from the law until all is fulfilled.

"Therefore whoever breaks one of the least of these commandments, and teaches men to do so, shall be called the lowest of all in the kingdom of heaven.

For I say to you that unless your goodness excels that of the scribes and the Pharisees, you shall never enter the kingdom of heaven.

"You have heard it said by men in the days of old, 'You shall not kill, and whoever kills shall be in danger of punishment.' But I say to you that whoever is angry with his brother without cause will be in danger of punishment by God. And whoever curses his brother shall be in danger of hell fire.

"Therefore, if you bring your offering to the altar, and there remember that your brother has any grievance against you, leave your offering there before the altar, and go and be first reconciled to your brother, and then come and make your offering.

"Agree with your adversary quickly while you are on the way to court with him, lest at any time the adversary deliver you to the judge, and the judge deliver you to the officer, and you be cast into prison. Truly I say to you, you shall never come out of there, till you have paid the last penny.

"Again, you have heard that it has been said by men of old, 'You shall

not swear falsely, but shall perform as you swear in your oaths.' But I say to you, swear not at all, neither by heaven, for it is God's throne, nor by earth, for it is his footstool; neither by Jerusalem, for it is the city of the great King. Nor shall you swear by your head, because you cannot make one hair white or black. But let what you have to say be simply 'Yes' or 'No,' for whatever is more than these comes from evil.

"You have heard that it has been said, 'An eye for an eye, a tooth for a tooth.' But I say to you, do not resist an injury. Whoever strikes you on the right cheek, turn to him also the other. If any man wants to sue you for your coat, let him have your cloak as well, and whoever compels you to go one mile, go with him two. Give to him that asks, and if anyone wishes to borrow from you, do not turn away.

THE LOVE OF ENEMIES

"You have heard that it has been said, 'You shall love your neighbor and hate your enemy.' But I say to you, love your enemies, bless those who curse you, do good to those who hate you, and pray for those who persecute you, so that you may be the children of your Father in heaven. For he makes his sun rise on the evil and on the good alike, and sends his rain on the just and on the unjust.

"For if you love those who love you, what reward do you deserve? Do not even tax-collectors do the same? And if you greet your brothers only, what do you do more than others? Do not even tax-collectors do so? Be therefore perfect, even as your Father who is in heaven is perfect.

"Take care that you do not do your good deeds before men, to be seen by them. Otherwise you will have no reward from your Father who is in heaven. When you give charity, do not sound a trumpet before yourself as the hypocrites do in the synagogues and in the streets, to have the praise of men. Truly I say to you, they have their reward in that. But when you give alms, let not your left hand know what your right hand does, so that your charity may be in secret. And your Father who sees what you do in secret shall reward you openly.

559

THE LORD'S PRAYER

"And when you pray, you shall not be as the hypocrites are, for they love to pray standing in the synagogues and on the corners of the streets, so that they may be seen by men. Truly I say to you: that is their reward. But you, when you pray, go into your room and when you have shut the door, pray to your Father who is unseen. And your Father who sees that which is in secret shall reward you openly.

"And when you pray, do not use idle phrases as the heathen do, for they think they shall be heard for their many words. Therefore do not be like them, for your Father knows everything you need, before you ask him. In this manner therefore pray:

"Our Father who art in heaven,
Hallowed be thy name.
Thy kingdom come.
Thy will be done on earth,
  as it is in heaven.
Give us this day our daily bread.
And forgive us our debts,
  as we forgive our debtors,
And lead us not into temptation,
  but deliver us from evil:
For thine is the kingdom, and the power,
  and the glory, for ever. Amen.

"For if you forgive men their offenses, your heavenly Father will also forgive you. But if you do not forgive men their offenses, neither will your Father forgive your offenses.

"Moreover, when you fast, do not look sad like the hypocrites. For they disfigure their faces so that they may appear to fast. Truly I say to you, they have their reward. But you, when you fast, anoint your head, and wash your face, so that you do not appear to fast to men, but to your Father. And your Father who sees that which is in secret shall reward you openly.

TREASURE IN HEAVEN

"Do not collect for yourselves treasures on earth, where moth and rust do damage, and where thieves break through and steal. But collect for yourselves treasures in heaven, where neither moth nor rust do damage, and where thieves do not break through and steal. For where your treasure is, there will be your heart also.

"The lamp of the body is the eye. If therefore your eye is sound, your whole

body shall be full of light. But if your eye is evil, your whole body shall be full of darkness. If therefore the light that is in you is darkness, how great is that darkness!

"No man can serve two masters, for either he will hate one and love the other, or else he will stand by one and despise the other. You cannot work for both God and worldly wealth. Therefore I say to you, do not worry about your well-being, what you shall eat, or what you shall drink, nor about your body and what you shall put on. Is not life more than food, and the body more than clothing?

"Behold the fowls of the air. They sow not, nor do they reap, nor gather into barns. Yet your heavenly Father feeds them. Are you not much better than they? Which of you by taking thought can add one minute to his life? And why do you worry about clothing? Consider the lilies of the field and how they grow. They do not work, nor do they spin. And yet I say to you that even Solomon in all his glory was not dressed like one of these. Therefore, if God so clothes the grass of

the field, which today grows and tomorrow is cast into the oven, shall he not much more clothe you, O you of little faith?

"Therefore do not worry saying, 'What shall we eat?' or 'What shall we drink?' or 'With what shall we be clothed?', for your heavenly Father knows that you need all these things. But seek first the kingdom of God, and his righteousness, and all these things shall be yours as well. Take therefore no thought for tomorrow, for tomorrow shall take care of itself. The troubles of today are enough for today.

"Judge not, that you be not judged. For by what judgement you make, you shall be judged, and with what measure you give, so shall you be measured. Why do you see the speck that is in your brother's eye, but do not notice the log that is in your own eye? How can you say to your brother, 'Let me pull out the speck from your eye,' when, behold, there is a log in your own eye? You hypocrite, first cast out the log from your own eye, and then you shall see clearly to cast out the speck from your brother's eye.

"Do not give that which is holy to the dogs, nor cast your pearls before swine, lest they trample them under their feet, and turn again and attack you.

"Ask, and it shall be given you. Seek, and you shall find. Knock, and it shall be opened to you. For every one that asks receives, and he that seeks finds, and to him that knocks it shall be opened. What man is there among you who, if his son asks bread, will give him a stone? Or if he ask a fish, will give him a serpent?

THE GOLDEN RULE

"If you then, being evil, know how to give good gifts to your children, how much more shall your Father who is in heaven give good things to them that ask him? Therefore, whatever you want that men should do to you, do so to them. For this is the law and the prophets.

"Enter in at the narrow gate, for wide is the gate and broad is the way that leads to destruction, and there are many who go in that way. Because narrow is the gate, and narrow is the way which leads to life, and there are few that find it.

BY THEIR FRUITS...

"Beware of false prophets which come to you in sheep's clothing, but inwardly are ravenous wolves. You shall know them by their fruits. Do men gather grapes from thorns, or figs from thistles? Every good tree brings forth good fruit, but a bad tree brings forth bad fruit. A good tree cannot bring forth bad fruit, nor can a bad tree bring forth good fruit. Every tree that does not bring forth good fruit is cut down, and cast into the fire. Therefore, by their fruits you shall know them.

"Not everyone that says to me, 'Lord, Lord,' shall enter into the kingdom of heaven, but he shall that does the will of my Father who is in heaven. Many will say to me that day, 'Lord, Lord, have we not prophesied in your name, and in your name cast out devils, and in your name done many wonderful works?' And then I will say to them, 'I never knew you. Depart from me, you that practice evil.'

"Therefore, whoever hears these sayings of mine, and does them, I will liken to a wise man who built his house upon a rock. The rain came down, and the floods came, and the winds blew and beat against that house, but it did not fall, for it was founded upon a rock. And every one that hears these sayings of mine and does them not, shall be like a foolish man who built his house upon the sand. And the rain came down, and the floods came, and the winds blew and beat against that house, and it fell. And great was the fall of it."

And it came to pass, when Jesus had ended these sayings, the people were astonished at his doctrine. For he taught them as one having authority, and not as the scribes.

THE MINISTRY OF JESUS CONTINUES

NOW when he had ended all his sayings in the audience of the people, he entered into Capernaum. There a certain centurion had a servant who was dear to him, who was sick and ready to die. And when he heard of Jesus, he sent to him the elders of the Jews, begging him to come and heal his servant. When the elders came to Jesus they spoke to him saying, "He deserves that you should do this, for he loves our nation and he has built us a synagogue."

Then Jesus went with them, and when he was not far from the house, the centurion sent friends to him, saying, "Lord, do not trouble yourself, for I am not worthy that you should enter my house, nor have I thought myself worthy to come to you. But say the word and my servant shall be healed. For I am a man of authority, having under me soldiers; I say to one, 'Go,' and he goes, and to another, 'Come,' and he comes, and to my servant, 'Do this,' and he does it."

When Jesus heard these things, he marveled, and, turning around, he said to the people that followed him, "I say to you, I have not found such great faith, no, not in Israel." And when they that were sent returned to the house they found the servant healed that had been sick.

JESUS HEALS THE WIDOW'S SON

The next day, he went into a city called Nain, and many of his disciples went with him and many people. Now when he came to the gate of the city, behold, there was a dead man being

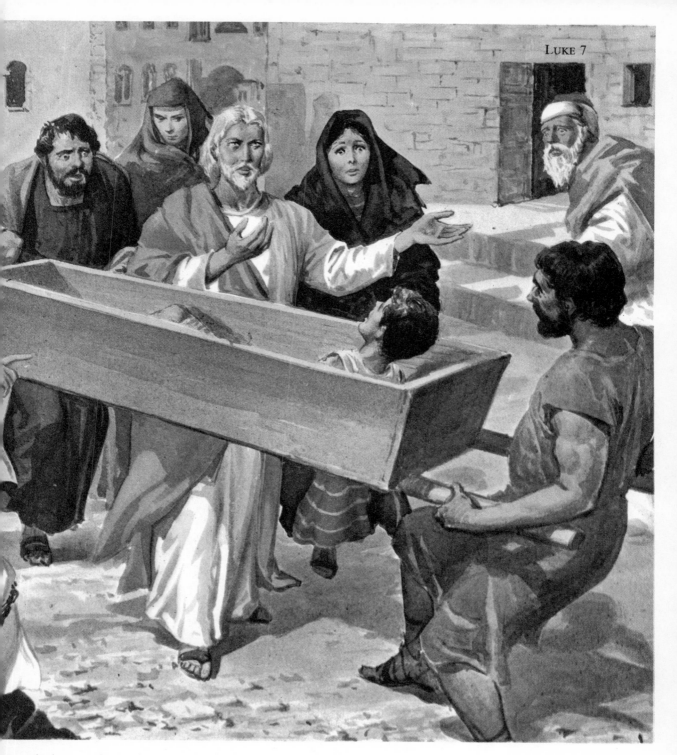

carried out, the only son of his mother who was a widow. And many people of the city were with her.

When the Lord saw her, he had compassion on her, and said to her, "Weep not." Then he went over and touched the coffin, while they that carried it stood still. And he said, "Young man, I say to you, arise." And he that was dead sat up and began to speak. And Jesus delivered him to his mother.

And there came a great fear on all, and they glorified God, saying that a great prophet has risen up among us, and that God has visited his people.

JESUS SENDS WORD TO JOHN THE BAPTIST

The disciples of John told him of all these things. And John called two of them and sent them to Jesus, saying, "Are you he that is to come, or are we to look for another?"

In the same hour when the men came, he cured many of their sicknesses and plagues, and evil spirits. Then Jesus answered:

"Go your way, and tell John what things you have seen and heard, how the blind see, the lame walk, the lepers are cleansed, the deaf hear, the dead are raised, and to the poor the gospel is preached. And blessed is he who shall not be offended by me."

When the messengers of John had departed, he began to speak to the people concerning John:

"What did you go into the wilderness to see? A reed shaken by the wind? What did you go out to discover? Behold, they who are gorgeously dressed and live delicately are in kings' courts. But what did you go out to see? A prophet? Yes, I say to you, and much more than a prophet. This is he of whom it is written: 'Behold, I send my messenger who shall prepare your way before you.' For I say to you, among those that are born of women there is not a greater prophet than John the Baptist. But he that is least in the kingdom of God is greater than he.

"To what therefore shall I compare the men of this generation? What are they like? They are like children sitting in the market place, and calling to one another and saying, 'We have piped for you, and you have not danced; we cried for you, and you have not wept.' For John the Baptist came neither eating bread nor drinking wine, and you say, 'He has a devil.' The Son of man has come eating and drinking, and you say, 'Behold, a gluttonous man and a drunkard, a friend of publicans and sinners.' "

ILLUSTRATED
GLOSSARY

Alms (p. 559)

An alms is money, food, or anything else given to the poor to relieve their need. Moses told his people to give to the poor and Jesus instructed people to show their love for one another by giving alms to the needy.

Baptism (p. 540)

The word "baptism" is from a Greek word that means "to dip or to put into water." At the time of Jesus, converts to Judaism were washed, or baptised, to signify their moral cleansing. When John baptised people, the outward cleansing represented an inner spiritual change.

Today Christians still practice baptism as an initiation into a higher spiritual life.

Caesar Augustus (p. 531)

Caesar Augustus was the first emperor of Rome. At birth he was called Octavius, but he later adopted the name of Augustus and added the family name of his granduncle, Julius Caesar. In time, "Caesar" came to mean emperor or king, and was used as the title of the Roman emperors.

Capernaum (p. 544)

Capernaum was a city in Galilee (see Galilee) on the northwestern shore of the Sea of Galilee. After Jesus left Nazareth (see Nazareth) the Gospels tell us he went to live in Capernaum by the sea. It was a busy city and fishing and trade were its principal industries. Unlike Nazareth, Capernaum was very hot in summer.

John the Baptist baptised Jesus in the Jordan River.

Centurion (p. 564)

A centurion was an officer in the Roman army and the leader of a century, a company of one hundred soldiers. The centurion was usually a Roman who rose from the ranks because of his good record as a soldier.

City of David (p. 531)

Although "City of David" is frequently used as a name for Jerusalem, here it refers to Bethlehem, the city where King David was born. Bethlehem is only five miles from Jerusalem.

Days of Purification (p. 532)

The time after a Jewish woman gave birth was called the days of purification. On the fortieth day after a boy was born and on the sixty-sixth after a girl was born, the mother went to the priest and offered a lamb for sacrifice. If she was poor, she offered two turtle doves or pigeons. Mary and Joseph were poor, so they offered two doves.

Fork is in his hand (p. 541)

This refers to the winnowing fork, which was used to toss grain into the air so the useless chaff would be blown away and separated from the good grain. The lines where these words appear use the language of reaping, threshing, and winnowing.

Galilee (p. 537)

Galilee, in Jesus' time, was a region of Palestine in the Roman province of Syria. Many small villages of the New Testament, such as Nazareth, Cana, Nain, Magdala, and Capernaum, were in Galilee.

Galilee was a pleasant region, with cool hills, lush valleys, and a shoreline on the Sea of Galilee. Agri-

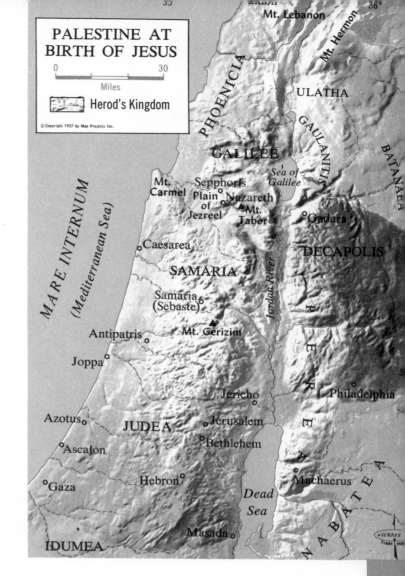

PALESTINE AT BIRTH OF JESUS

0   30
Miles

Herod's Kingdom

© Copyright 1957 by Map Projects Inc.

culture flourished on the Plain of Jezreel where grain, grapes, olives and dates were grown. The Sea of Galilee was a center for the fishing industry. Fish were sold locally, or salted and sent to other places. Shipping was easy, for a number of caravan routes passed through Galilee.

Gentiles (p. 532)

To the Jews, Gentiles were people who were not Jewish. The first Christians were almost all Jews; later, Gentiles were accepted into Christianity. Today the term Gentile is often used to mean a Christian.

Gospel (p. 566)

The word gospel comes from two Old English words, "god" and "spell." God meant good and spell meant news. Many Christian writings were once called gospels, because they told of the "good news" of Jesus. Now the word is generally used for the accounts of Jesus written by Matthew, Mark, Luke and John.

Herod, Tetrarch of Galilee (p. 540)

Herod Antipas, son of Herod the Great, was made ruler of Galilee when his father died, and was given the title of tetrarch. Jesus called Herod "that fox," meaning that he was sly and treacherous. He ruled until A.D. 39.

Herod the Great (p. 526)

Herod the Great was made ruler of Palestine by its Roman conquerors in 37 B.C., and he ruled until 4 B.C. During this time he was given the title of King of Judea by Caesar Augustus. (See Caesar Augustus.)

Because Herod was an Edomite, a traditional enemy of the Israelites, he was disliked by the Jewish people. He tried to please them by rebuilding their temple, but he taxed them so heavily to do so that he only added to their dislike.

Though he made efforts to please, Herod was often a cruel man. He killed many members of his own family.

His forefather David (p. 528)

Jesus was of the family of King David.

John the Son of Zacharias (p. 540)

John is more commonly known as John the Baptist. He led a strict life and may have been a Nazirite, a person who devoted himself entirely to God. As signs of their devotion, Nazirites neither cut their hair nor drank wine. John also wore poor clothing and ate a meager diet.

Lilies of the field (p. 561)

Today scholars believe these flowers were not lilies but scarlet anemones or windflowers, which still grow wild in fields of the Holy Land. Or the flowers might have been common daisies or asphodels. Jesus also may not have meant a particular flower, but all the wildflowers of his homeland.

Manger (p. 531)

A manger was a trough, usually made of stone, from which farm animals ate. The farmer filled the manger with straw for his cattle and donkeys.

Nazareth (p. 537)

Nazareth was a quiet town built on a plateau about 15 miles west of the Sea of Galilee. Its people were known as strict followers of the law of Moses. In fact, the town's name was taken from Hebrew words that mean "consecrated people." Jesus grew to manhood in Nazareth.

Pharisees (p. 550)

The Pharisees were a group of devout Jews who were civic leaders. They became active about 200 B.C. The Pharisees carefully obeyed the Mosaic Law and also gave strict attention to the details of other rules that had been handed down by word of mouth. They objected to Israel making friends with other countries. The people respected the Pharisees, probably because of their devoutness. Most of the scribes were Pharisees.

Pontius Pilate (p. 540)

Pontius Pilate was made procurator, or manager, of Judea by Tiberius Caesar in A.D. 26. (See Tiberius Caesar.) He was not a successful ruler because he did nothing to win over the Jewish people. Even Herod Agrippa, grandson of Herod the Great, described Pilate as cruel, stubborn, and violent. He was called back to Rome in A.D. 36.

Publicans (p. 566)

See Tax-collectors.

Sadducees (p. 540)

The Sadducees were a group of aristocratic religious Jews who became leaders about the same time as the Pharisees. (See Pharisees.) The beliefs of the two groups were quite different. The Sadducees followed the written law of Moses with care, but did not believe in the traditional laws that had been handed down by their ancestors. Unlike the Pharisees, they believed in

forming alliances with foreign lands. Both the Pharisees and the Sadducees were opposed to their Roman rulers.

Show yourself to the priest (p. 549)

According to Mosaic Law, a person who believed he had been cured of leprosy had to appear before the priests. They would examine him to decide if he had really been healed. The law of Moses also required those who had been cured to make offerings of thanks to the Lord.

Swaddling clothes (p. 531)

In Eastern lands, babies were wrapped with narrow bands of cloth called swaddling clothes.

Synagogue (p. 548)

When the Jews were taken into exile in Babylon, they met in private homes to pray and to study the Scriptures. From these gatherings came the idea of the synagogue, a meeting place. When the Jews returned to their homeland, they built synagogues in their towns and cities.

The sacred scrolls were kept in the synagogue and the people met there on the Sabbath to pray and hear the scriptures read aloud. The Scriptures were also read on festival days and on Mondays and Thursdays, the market days, so the farmers who could not travel on the Sabbath could hear the Scriptures read and interpreted.

Tax-collectors (p. 541)

The Romans imposed very heavy taxes on the people of Palestine. This money was collected by local Jews acting as tax-collectors, or publicans. They were scorned by the community for serving the Romans and were generally considered to be dishonest.

John warned the tax-collectors: "Collect no more than you are expected to." Probably some of the tax-collectors cheated by collecting too much and keeping the difference.

Tiberius Caesar (p. 540)

Tiberius Caesar, the adopted son of Caesar Augustus, became Emperor of Rome in A.D. 14. It was he who appointed Pontius Pilate to office. (See Pontius Pilate.)

Under a bushel (p. 558)

To put a light under a bushel meant to put it under a basket where it could not be seen.

Wise men from the east (p. 534)

The wise men were probably students of astrology who had been watching the skies when they saw the star that led them to Bethlehem.

Zacharias (p. 526)

Zacharias was a member of the tribe of Levi, so he was eligible to serve as a priest in the temple. At that time there were thousands of priests, and not every priest was able to offer sacrifice. Zacharias was one of the privileged ones.

In those days, it was the custom for the priest to go outside of the temple after the service and to bless the people. That is why a crowd was waiting for Zacharias.

E
T THE
ESUS

|_____| 300

ads
ea routes

RAETIA
NORICUM
ALPS
PANNONIA
ILLYRICUM
Danube R.
DACIA
Mare Hadriaticum
MOESIA
THRACIA
PONTUS EUXINUS
(Black Sea)
Byzantium
CORSICA
Rome
Ostia
SARDINIA
Mare Tyrrhenum
MACEDONIA
Thessalonica
ACHAIA
Mare Aegaeum
BITHYNIA ET PONTUS
GALATIA
CAPPADOCIA
Actium
Pergamum
ASIA
Smyrna
Ephesus
Miletus
CILICIA E
Tarsus
Rhegium
SICILIA
Athenae
Corinthus
Sparta
Rhodes
LYCIA
RHODES
CYPRUS
Dam
M A R E
(Mediterranean Sea)
I N T E R N U M
Carthage
Cnossus
CRETA
Caesarea
Na
Seb
Jerusalem
Bethle
AFRICA
CYRENAICA
Alexandria
Memphis
AEGYPTUS